A TRUE BOOK™

The Bald Eagle

ELAINE LANDAU

Children's Press®
A Division of Scholastic Inc.
New York   Toronto   London   Auckland   Sydney
Mexico City   New Delhi   Hong Kong
Danbury, Connecticut

Content Consultant

David R. Smith, PhD

Academic Adviser and Adjunct Assistant Professor of History

University of Michigan–Ann Arbor

Reading Consultant

Cecilia Minden-Cupp, PhD

Early Literacy Consultant and Author

Library of Congress Cataloging-in-Publication Data

Landau, Elaine.
The Bald eagle / by Elaine Landau.
    p. cm.—(A true book)
Includes bibliographical references and index.
ISBN-13: 978-0-531-12626-4 (lib. bdg.)   978-0-531-14776-4 (pbk.)
ISBN-10: 0-531-12626-9 (lib. bdg.)   0-531-14776-2 (pbk.)
1. Bald eagle—Juvenile literature. 2. Bald eagle—United
States—Juvenile literature. I. Title. II. Series.
QL696.F32L33 2007
598.9'43—dc22   2007009051

Find the Truth!

Everything you are about to read is true *except* for one of the sentences on this page.

Which one is **TRUE**?

T or F Bald eagles are skilled hunters.

T or F There are fewer than 1,000 bald eagles left in the United States today.

Find the answer in this book.

3

Contents

THE **BIG** TRUTH!

Size of the Bald Eagle

The words *E Pluribus Unum* are on the Great Seal. This is Latin for "out of many, one".

In the wild, bald eagles typically live about 20–30 years, but can live as long as 50 years.

CHAPTER 1

A Powerful Symbol

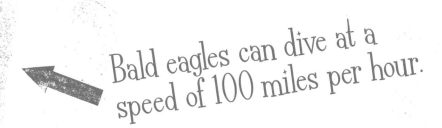

Bald eagles can dive at a speed of 100 miles per hour.

Think of a large, strong, beautiful bird. It soars through the sky. Are you imagining a bald eagle?

The bald eagle is a **symbol** of the United States. A symbol is an object that stands for something else. Eagles have been used as symbols of power in different parts of the world. Read on to find out why.

People have admired eagles for thousands of years. Ancient Romans admired the courage and power of the eagle. Roman soldiers carried eagles made of silver into battle. They wanted to be strong and fearless like the eagle. They placed their silver eagles high on poles. The sight made the Romans proud. It also scared their enemies.

This metal eagle was created for the Roman army between the first and third centuries A.D.

Who Else Likes Eagles?

Countries all around the world have used the eagle on their **coats of arms**. A coat of arms is a design that stands for a country, family, or group.

- **Germany** has used the eagle as a symbol for more than 3,000 years!

- **Mexico's** coat of arms has hardly changed in hundreds of years. It features an eagle grasping a snake.

These images show coats of arms from Germany (top) and Mexico (bottom).

- **Nigeria** has the eagle on its coat of arms to show strength.

- **Poland's** white eagle stands for victory and power.

9

John J. Audubon, a famous naturalist, named a species of eagles found in Alaska after George Washington. It is called the *washingtoniensis* species.

CHAPTER 2

The King of Birds

The largest bald eagles in the United States are in Alaska.

People use eagles as a symbol of strength. Eagles may also stand for other things, such as victory or freedom. Why might people choose eagles over other animals? What are eagles really like?

The symbol of the United States Marine Corps includes an eagle standing on a globe with an anchor.

11

A booted eagle looks on from its perch in an evergreen tree.

Eagles are part of a group of birds called **raptors**. Raptors are birds that hunt other animals for food. Owls and hawks are also raptors.

There are 59 different **species**, or types, of eagles. The harpy eagle is the largest species of eagle. Harpy eagles can weigh up to 25 pounds (11 kilograms). They live in South America. These eagles eat monkeys and other small animals. One of the smallest species is the booted eagle. These eagles weigh about 2 pounds (0.9 kg). They hunt mostly mice and small lizards.

What Are Eagles Like?

Most eagles are large birds. Adult eagles can grow as tall as 3 feet (0.9 meter). That is as tall as some preschoolers! When an eagle spreads its wings, it really looks huge. The largest eagles can have a **wingspan** of up to 8 feet (2.4 m). Wingspan is the distance between the tips of the wings when they are fully spread.

These long, powerful wings make eagles great flyers. Eagles have been spotted flying over high mountaintops. These birds seem to rule the sky. No wonder nations have chosen them as a symbol for their armies.

A bald eagle flies above mountains in Alaska.

Eagles are also skilled hunters. They have strong feet and beaks. Their feet have **talons**, or sharp claws. Excellent eyesight helps eagles spot their next meal. Then they swoop down through the air. They grab their **prey** with their talons. Eagles can carry an animal through the air for miles before they stop and eat it.

Like all birds, eagles don't have teeth to chew their food. They hold the animal with one or both feet and rip it apart with their powerful beak. Then they gulp it down.

Strong, sharp talons help eagles grab prey and hold onto it as they fly. Talons help them hold onto branches, as well.

A bald eagle in mid-flight uses its talons to feed itself a fish.

What Are Bald Eagles Like?

Don't let its name fool you. The bald eagle is not really bald. It is a large brown bird with white feathers on its head. How did it get its name? The word *bald* comes from an old word *balled*, which means "shining white." People used the word to describe the white feathers on the eagle's head.

There's something special about bald eagles to Americans. The bald eagle is found only in North America. It lives as far north as Alaska. Bald eagles have also been seen as far south as Mexico. These birds live in every state except Hawaii.

It is illegal to keep a bald eagle as a pet.

A bald eagle soars on thermals, or pockets of warm air created by heat from the sun.

Bald eagles usually lay two or three eggs in the spring. Female chicks are larger than male chicks.

Bald eagle chicks are mostly brownish-gray. It takes three years for any feathers to turn white.

A bald eagle's wingspan can reach about 7 feet (2.1 m). Males can weigh as much as 9 pounds (4.1 kg). The female bald eagle is heavier than the male. It can weigh 15 pounds (6.8 kg)!

Bald eagles build huge nests out of tree branches. The nests can be as big as 6 feet (2 m) across. Bald eagles often nest in tall trees near rivers. A male and a female eagle build a nest together. The same two eagles will return to their nest every spring.

Bald eagles eat fish. They can sit in a tree for hours waiting to spot a fish. Then they grab it in a flash! Eagles will eat many other kinds of animals if they can't find fish.

Bald eagle parents will fiercely defend their chicks from all lurking predators. This male protects its eaglet.

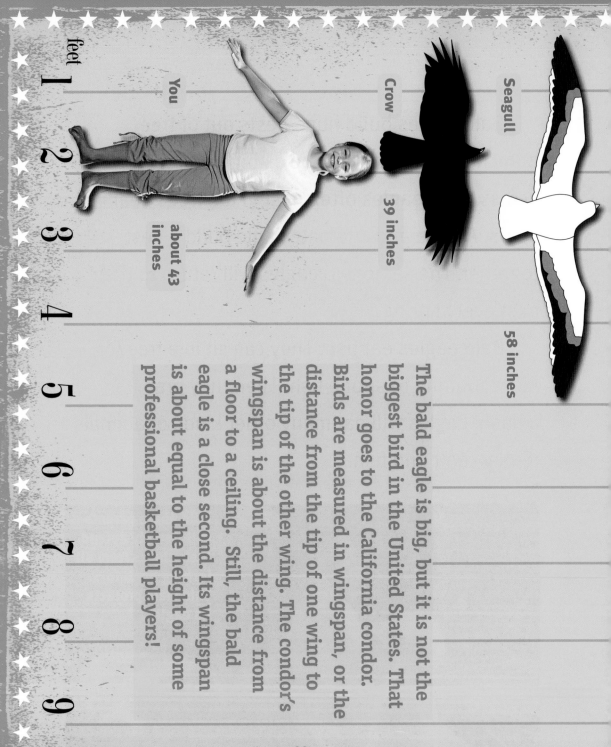

feet

1
2
3
4
5
6
7
8
9

You

about 43 inches

Crow

39 inches

Seagull

58 inches

The bald eagle is big, but it is not the biggest bird in the United States. That honor goes to the California condor. Birds are measured in wingspan, or the distance from the tip of one wing to the tip of the other wing. The condor's wingspan is about the distance from a floor to a ceiling. Still, the bald eagle is a close second. Its wingspan is about equal to the height of some professional basketball players!

Size of the Bald Eagle

Bald Eagle

7 feet

Adult Condor

9 feet

The first battle of the Revolutionary War was fought in Lexington, Massachusetts, on April 19, 1775.

CHAPTER 3

A New Nation's Needs

No one knows for sure who fired the first shot of the Revolutionary War.

The United States wasn't an independent country before 1776. It was a group of colonies ruled by Great Britain. Americans wanted to form their own nation. So they fought the **Revolutionary War** against Britain for several years. Finally, America won its freedom.

The young country formed a government and chose their new leaders. Three of the most important leaders were Thomas Jefferson, John Adams, and Benjamin Franklin.

The new government needed a **seal**. This seal was a special stamp. Leaders needed to stamp official government letters and papers. The stamp would let people know that the papers were really from the government. Franklin, Adams, and Jefferson were chosen to design the seal.

What would the seal look like? People came up with many different ideas. For a while, it seemed as if no one could agree.

John Adams and Thomas Jefferson both died on July 4, 1826, exactly fifty years after signing the Declaration of Independence.

Benjamin Franklin (left), John Adams (center), and Thomas Jefferson (right) helped to write the document that first declared the United States a free country. The document was the Declaration of Independence, written in 1776.

Ideas, Ideas, Ideas

Franklin wanted to show the story from the Bible of Moses parting the Red Sea. Jefferson chose another Bible story. Adams wanted to show a Greek hero named Hercules. Which idea did the other leaders select? None of them! The new government instead chose a new group of people to design the seal.

Hercules is a popular hero in Greek mythology. He is known for his great strength and bravery. In this painting, he is shown slaying a hydra, a huge snake with many heads.

Charles Thomson served as secretary for the top levels of American government, from 1774 to 1789.

One of these people was Charles Thomson. He and his friend, William Barton, worked together on the design. Barton was a young lawyer from Philadelphia. He came up with the idea of using the bald eagle. He believed that the bird represented leadership and power.

Thomson is one of only 2 men to have signed the original version of the Declaration of Independence.

After this design for the Great Seal was approved, it was engraved into brass. Then it could be printed on documents again and again.

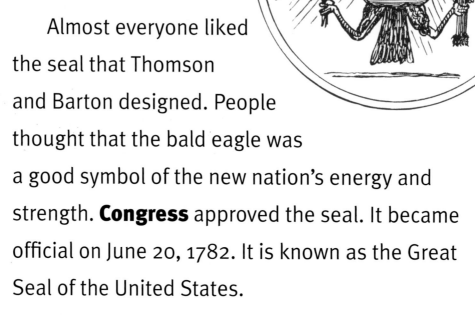

Almost everyone liked the seal that Thomson and Barton designed. People thought that the bald eagle was a good symbol of the new nation's energy and strength. **Congress** approved the seal. It became official on June 20, 1782. It is known as the Great Seal of the United States.

The wings of a bald eagle stretch from one edge of the Great Seal to the other. The eagle grasps 13 arrows, for the 13 original states, in one of its claws. The arrows show that Americans will fight for their freedom.

The eagle holds an olive branch in its other claw. The olive branch is a symbol of peace. The eagle faces the olive branch, showing that the United States prefers peace to war.

In the center of the Great Seal is a red-and white-striped shield. The shield has 13 stripes. The United States had only 13 states when the Great Seal was created. The 13 stripes stand for these states.

The Great Seal is used to make the president's signature official.

An eagle tops a totem pole in British Columbia, Canada. The bald eagle is a powerful symbol for many Native Americans.

CHAPTER 4

A Perfect Match

Some Native Americans carve images of eagles on totem poles.

So how was the bald eagle chosen to be our national symbol? Congress talked about it for six years. Everyone agreed that the symbol should be an animal from North America.

The bald eagle is a majestic symbol of American strength and freedom.

31

Majesty and Freedom

Freedom was also very important to congressional leaders. Many Americans had given their lives to help the country win its freedom from Great Britain. Americans were proud of their courage and strength. The national symbol needed to stand for Americans' will to be free.

The bald eagle was a perfect match. Eagles soar freely above the mountain peaks. Their excellent eyesight allows them to see things from very far away. Strong countries need good vision. Leaders need to see problems clearly.

Wild turkeys can fly more than 55 miles per hour.

Our National Turkey?

Not everyone approved of the country's national symbol. Benjamin Franklin preferred the wild turkey to the bald eagle. He pointed out that eagles steal food from other birds, while turkeys are very brave.

Franklin put his thoughts in a letter to his daughter in 1784. "For my own part," he wrote, "I wish the Bald Eagle had not been chosen the representative of our country. . . . He does not get his living honestly. . . . The Turkey is in comparison a much more respectable bird, and a true original Native of America."

The male wild turkey's head and neck are brilliantly colored with red, white, and blue, the official colors of the United States flag.

Congress also liked the bald eagle's strength and size. They agreed it was a beautiful bird. They made the bald eagle the national symbol in 1789.

The United States was a smaller country in 1789. It had fewer people. Bald eagles had room to fly and nest. Scientists think there were about 100,000 bald eagles at the time.

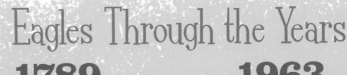

Eagles Through the Years

1789
Some 100,000 bald eagles live in North America.

1963
Fewer than 1,000 bald eagles are left in the United States.

1940
The Bald Eagle Protection Act is passed. This makes it illegal to kill bald eagles.

The country's growing population created problems for the bald eagle. People built homes where forests and fields used to be. Power lines, airplanes, and **pesticides** used to kill insects accidentally killed eagles. By 1963, fewer than 1,000 bald eagles were left in the United States.

Then, Americans began to protect bald eagles. Today, about 20,000 are living in the United States.

1972
The most deadly pesticides are banned.

1973
President Richard Nixon signs the Endangered Species Act.

1978
Bald eagles are put on the Endangered Species list.

2007
Bald eagles are doing so well that they are taken off the endangered species list.

A bald eagle uses its keen eyesight to look for prey.

CHAPTER 5

Eagles All Around

 A bald eagle can see twice as sharp as a person can.

Pictures of the bald eagle are everywhere. The bald eagle is on stamps, coins, and the one-dollar bill. Many companies use the bald eagle on signs and in advertisements. The bald eagle reminds people of the ideals on which the United States was founded.

The bald eagle has been on the back of the $1 coin since it was first made in 1794.

UNITED STATES OF AMERICA · 1 OZ. FINE SILVER~ONE DOLLAR

From Badges to the Moon

The bald eagle is a common symbol in the U.S. government. It is on more than just the Great Seal. The bird is on the official seals of the Supreme Court and the president. When the president makes an important speech from the Oval Office, you can see the bald eagle on television. The presidential seal hangs on the front of the presidential podium.

The bald eagle is on the front of the U.S. Navy Department's official seal.

An eagle rides on the tail of this Air Force fighter jet.

The U.S. military uses a symbol similar to the one the ancient Romans used. An eagle is part of the **insignia**, or official badge, for captains of the U.S. Navy, Marines, Air Force, and Coast Guard.

This photo is of Old Abe, the bald eagle carried into battle by Union soldiers in the Civil War. During the war, Southern troops tried unsuccessfully to capture the eagle.

In Wartime

The bald eagle was an important symbol for the United States during the Civil War in the 1860s. Southern states formed their own country. States from the North fought to keep the United States together. Northern soldiers from Wisconsin brought a live eagle into battle!

These soldiers named the eagle Old Abe, after President Abraham Lincoln. Old Abe inspired the soldiers to fight bravely. He stood by the American flag during more than 30 battles.

"The Eagle Has Landed"

In 1969, the United States launched a rocket into space. The rocket carried three Americans through space for many days. Then these astronauts climbed into a small landing craft named *Eagle*. The whole world watched as the *Eagle* dropped toward the moon. "The Eagle has landed," said astronaut Neil Armstrong. Then he opened the door and became the first person to step onto the moon.

Buzz Aldrin walks on the surface of the moon during the *Apollo 11* mission, with the *Eagle* spacecraft in the background.

The bald eagle has been with the United States since the country was born. The bird flew over rivers and fields. The symbol was stamped onto some of the government's first letters. Americans now protect the bald eagle. They want to make sure the bird doesn't die out.

Americans also work to protect the ideas that the eagle stands for. They work to keep America strong and free. ★

When flying, bald eagles use their tails to change direction and to glide on drafts of air.

Scientific name: *Haliaeetus leucocephalus*

Wingspan: About 7 ft. (2.1 m)

Maximum weight: 9 lbs (4.1 kg) for males; 15 lbs (6.8 kg) for females

Maximum speed: 44 mi. (71 km) per hour in flight; 100 mi. (161 km) per hour, diving

Average life span in the wild: 25 years

Maximum life span: about 50 years

Diet: Fish, small mammals, waterbirds, wading birds, and carrion (dead animal matter)

Live: Near water

Range: Canada, every U.S. state except Hawaii

Population in 1782: About 100,000

Population in 1963: Less than 1,000

Population in 2007: About 20,000

Did you find the truth?

T Bald eagles are skilled hunters.

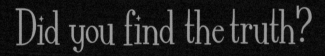

F There are fewer than 1,000 bald eagles left in the United States today.

Resources

Books

Becker, John E. *The Bald Eagle*. San Diego: KidHaven Press, 2002.

Binns, Tristan Boyer. *The Bald Eagle*. Chicago: Heinemann Library, 2001.

Collard, Sneed B., III. *Birds of Prey: A Look at Daytime Raptors*. Danbury, CT: Franklin Watts, 1999.

Dell, Pamela. *The Bald Eagle*. Minneapolis: Compass Point Books, 2004.

Jango-Cohen, Judith. *The Bald Eagle*. Minneapolis: Lerner Publications, 2003.

Marcovitz, Hal. *The Bald Eagle*. Philadelphia: Mason Crest, 2003.

Martin-James, Kathleen. *Soaring Bald Eagles*. Minneapolis: Lerner Publications, 2001.

Pearl, Norman. *The Bald Eagle*. Minneapolis: Picture Window Books, 2007.

Wilcox, Charlotte. *Bald Eagles*. Minneapolis: Carolrhoda Books, 2003.

Organizations and Web Sites

American Bald Eagle Information
www.baldeagleinfo.com
Look for lots of links and some interesting photos.

American Eagle Foundation
www.eagles.org
Sign up to win an eagle visit to your school.

Vermont Bald Eagle Restoration Initiative
www.cvps.com/eagles/nationalbird.shtml
Click on the Gallery link for bald eagle photos.

Places to Visit

**San Diego Zoo's
Wild Animal Park**
15500 San Pasqual Valley Road
Escondido, CA 92027-7017
760-747-8702
www.sandiegozoo.org/wap/
index.html
Visit the Condor Ridge area to
see a bald eagle.

Important Words

coats of arms – designs that stand for a country, family, or group

Congress – the highest lawmaking body of the United States, made up of the Senate and the House of Representatives

insignia (in-SIG-nee-uh) – a badge or design that can show a person's rank or membership in an organization

pesticides (PESS-tuh-sidez) – chemicals used to kill insects that harm crops

prey – an animal killed as food by another animal

raptors – birds that hunt other animals for food

Revolutionary War – a war from 1775 to 1783 that gave the 13 American colonies independence from Great Britain, forming the United States of America

seal – a special stamp that is a symbol or mark of office

species (SPEE-seez) – a group of animals or plants that are similar and have a common name

symbol (SIM-bul) – an object that stands for something else

talons – sharp claws of a bird that hunts other animals

wingspan – the distance between the tips of the wings when fully spread

Index

About the Author

Award-winning author Elaine Landau has written more than 300 books for children and young adults. She worked as a newspaper reporter, a children's book editor, and a youth services librarian before becoming a full-time writer.

Ms. Landau lives in Miami, Florida, with her husband and their son, Michael. She enjoys writing about history and often visits the places she writes about. You can visit her at her Web site: www.elainelandau.com.